Pearson
Revise

T0351913

Revise BTEC Tech Award

Digital Information Technology (2022)

Practice Assessments Plus⁺

Series Consultant: Harry Smith

Author: Colin Harber-Stuart

A note from the publisher

While the publishers have made every attempt to ensure that advice on the qualification and its assessment is accurate, the official specification and associated assessment guidance materials are the only authoritative source of information and should always be referred to for definitive guidance.

This qualification is reviewed on a regular basis and may be updated in the future.

Any such updates that affect the content of this Revision Guide will be outlined at

www.pearsonfe.co.uk/BTECchanges. The eBook version of this Revision Guide will also be updated to reflect the latest guidance as soon as possible.

Published by Pearson Education Limited, 80 Strand, London, WC2R ORL.

www.pearsonschoolsandfecolleges.co.uk

Copies of official specifications for all Pearson qualifications may be found on the website: qualifications.pearson.com

Text and illustrations © Pearson Education Ltd 2022

Typeset, produced and illustrated by PDQ Media

Cover illustration © Simple Line/Shutterstock

The right of Colin Harber-Stuart to be identified as author of this work has been asserted by him in accordance with the Copyright, Designs and Patents Act 1988.

First published 2022

25 24

10 9 8 7 6 5

British Library Cataloguing in Publication Data

A catalogue record for this book is available from the British Library

ISBN 978 1 292 43622 7

Printed by Ashford Colour Press Ltd

Notes from the publisher

1. While the publishers have made every attempt to ensure that advice on the qualification and its assessment is accurate, the official specification and associated assessment guidance materials are the only authoritative source of information and should always be referred to for definitive guidance.

Pearson examiners have not contributed to any sections in this resource relevant to examination papers for which they have responsibility.

2. Pearson has robust editorial processes, including answer and fact checks, to ensure the accuracy of the content in this publication, and every effort is made to ensure this publication is free of errors. We are, however, only human, and occasionally errors do occur. Pearson is not liable for any misunderstandings that arise as a result of errors in this publication, but it is our priority to ensure that the content is accurate. If you spot an error, please do contact us at resourcescorrections@pearson.com so we can make sure it is corrected.

Websites

Pearson Education Limited is not responsible for the content of any external internet sites. It is essential for tutors to preview each website before using it in class so as to ensure that the URL is still accurate, relevant and appropriate. We suggest that tutors bookmark useful websites and consider enabling students to access them through the school/college intranet.

Introduction

This book has been designed to help you to practise the skills you may need for the external assessment of BTEC Tech Award **Digital Information Technology**, Component 3: Effective Digital Working Practices.

About the practice assessments

The book contains four practice assessments for the component. Unlike your actual assessment, the questions have targeted hints, guidance and support in the margin to help you understand how to tackle them:

 links to relevant pages in the BTEC Tech Award Digital Information Technology Revision Guide, so you can revise the essential content. This will also help you to understand how the essential content is applied to different contexts when assessed.

 to get you started and remind you of the skills or knowledge you need to apply.

 to help you on how to approach a question, such as making a brief plan.

 to provide content that you need to learn, such as a definition or policy.

 to help you avoid common pitfalls.

 to remind you of content related to the question to aid your revision on that topic.

 for use with the final practice assessment to help you become familiar with answering in a given time and ways to think about allocating time for different questions.

There is space for you to write your answers to the questions in this book. However, if you require more space to complete your answers, you may want to use separate paper.

There is also an answer section at the back of the book, so you can check your answers for each practice assessment.

Check the Pearson website

For overarching guidance on the official assessment outcomes and key terms used in your assessment, please refer to the specification on the Pearson website. For this component, check whether the assessment is completed on a computer.

The practice questions, support and answers in this book are provided to help you to revise the essential content in the specification, along with ways of applying your skills. Details of your actual assessment may change, so always make sure you are up to date on its format and requirements by asking your tutor or checking the Pearson website for the most up-to-date Sample Assessment Material, Mark Schemes and any past papers.

Contents

A small bit of small print

Practice assessment 1

Revision Guide
pages 22 and
30

> **Answer ALL questions.**
> **Write your answers in the spaces provided.**

1 A cinema sells tickets on its website.

(a) The website has recently been a victim of a malware attack.

State **two** reasons why digital systems are attacked.

1 ....

....

2 ....

....

2 marks

(b) The cinema has installed anti-virus software to protect against loss of data from a further malware attack.

Explain **one** other benefit of using anti-virus software.

....

....

....

....

2 marks

Hint

State questions expect you to recall one or more pieces of information.

Hint

When asked to **state** two reasons, write a short statement for each. You don't need to include a lot of detail.

Hint

Explain questions require you to support your point with a linked reason.

Hint

When you **explain** a benefit, give a reason why or how something will improve a situation. For example, a spam filter directs emails containing spam into a separate folder, reducing the time spent reading unwanted messages.

Watch out!

In 1(b), you are given some information and then asked to provide one other piece of information. Make sure you give different information to what's in the question.

Watch out!

Anti-virus software is often provided as part of a larger suite of security software. Make sure you do not confuse it with other types of security software, such as firewalls or anti-spam protection.

Hint

Identify questions may ask you to select the correct information from a list or source.

Hint

If you are not sure which two items are correct, you could start by identifying which items you know are not correct. This will reduce the number of items from which to select your answer.

Hint

In Question 1(d), you need to give one feature of a strong password and explain how this feature will make the system more secure.

Prepare

It will help you to think why this password is weak and what the features of a strong password are. Adding any one of these features will make the password stronger.

(c) The cinema secures its digital systems by restricting access to its offices.

Identify **two** methods that will restrict physical access to unauthorised users.

2 marks

Tick the boxes.

☐ Disable autocompletion during data entry

☐ Door locks

☐ Encryption

☐ Anti-virus software

☐ Firewall

☐ Swipe card

(d) Suchitra has been employed by the cinema to update the website. She is asked to create a password on the system. She chooses 'secret'.

Explain how she could make the password stronger.

....

....

....

....

2 marks

(e) The cinema regularly requires staff to change their passwords.

Explain **two** benefits to the cinema of staff regularly changing their passwords.

1 ....

....

....

....

2 ....

....

....

....

| 4 marks |

| Total for Question 1 = 12 marks |

Revision Guide
page 34

Hint

When you **explain** you need to give clear details and a reason for each benefit you select. For example, if your answer is that the data will be more secure, you need to give a reason why the benefit will help the cinema.

Hint

You are asked for **two** benefits. Do not give more than two as you will not get any more marks.

Watch out!

Make sure you read the question carefully. The benefits must be for the cinema. You will not get marks for writing about benefits to the customer.

Watch out!

The question asks for benefits. Don't give drawbacks!

Explore

According to a survey in 2018, most people do not change their passwords unless prompted. Most also use the same password on more than one account. Commonly used passwords include '123456' and 'password'!

Revision Guide
pages 23 and
48

Hint

When answering this **state** question, you only need to recall two data protection principles. You do not need to go into any detail or give more than two responses.

Watch out!

There are six data protection principles, but only some of them apply to the collection of personal data. Make sure you do not state principles that apply to data storage or processing.

 Explore

Health-care and biometric data are unique to each individual and can be used to identify them.

Hint

In this **explain** question, you need to identify an appropriate course of action and then explain it, giving a reason how or why it would have the intended effect.

Watch out!

In 2(b), your explanation must relate to the course of action you have stated. For example, if the action is 'Delete the file', your explanation must explain how deleting it will protect the system from harm.

2 An online clothing retailer collects personal data when customers purchase products from its website.

(a) The retailer needs to comply with data protection principles when collecting data.

State **two** data protection principles that apply to the collection of data.

1 ....

....

2 ....

....

2 marks

(b) An employee receives an email with an attachment from an unknown sender.

Explain what the employee should do to reduce the threat of a malware attack on the retailer's digital systems.

....

....

....

....

2 marks

(c) The clothing website uses features to aid accessibility.

Annotate the web page by:

- identifying and labelling two different accessibility features of this website
- stating how each feature aids accessibility.

4 marks

An example has been provided.

What to Wear – ethical fashion for everyone!

Selling responsibly sourced clothing since 2009

A shop clothing rail displaying a variety of ladies tops

AA_A

Adjustable font size. Enables users with visual impairments to read text more easily.

Revision Guide
page 17

Hint

Annotate questions require you to label a diagram and provide an explanation for each feature you identify, as shown in the example given.

Hint

To annotate you need to select a feature on the web page that will aid accessibility, then explain how it will do this, for example what the feature does and how it might benefit. Draw an arrow pointing from your explanation towards the feature.

Hint

Make sure you only add two annotations to the diagram. Do not repeat the example in the question.

Watch out!

Some parts of this web page will **not** aid accessibility, so make sure you know about the main accessibility features of web pages.

Revision Guide
page 35

Hint

Make a list of possible benefits of having an acceptable software policy. Then think of reasons why some of them will benefit the retailer. For example, the retailer could include video games in a list of unauthorised software which may help workers to be less distracted at work.

Watch out!

An acceptable software policy is not the same as an acceptable use policy. Make sure you are clear about the differences as each will have different benefits.

Watch out!

Remember to focus on benefits to the retailer. The question is not asking you to discuss drawbacks or the impact on customers.

(d) Staff using the retailer's digital systems must follow its acceptable software policy.

Explain **two** benefits to the retailer of having an acceptable software policy.

1 ....

....

....

....

2 ....

....

....

....

4 marks

Total for Question 2 = 12 marks

3 A company designs and makes greetings cards which it sells through its high-street shops.

(a) The company stores its data in files on its digital systems at head office. The data in each file is encrypted.

Explain **one** way that data encryption increases the security of data stored in files.

....

....

....

....

2 marks

Revision Guide
page 31

Hint

Start by identifying a feature of data encryption. Then explain how this feature will help the business keep data secure.

Hint

You need to show that you understand what 'encryption' means by using another word with the same meaning. You do not need to explain how encryption works.

Watch out!

The question is about data that is saved on a network storage device. Avoid writing about how encryption helps data being transmitted.

LEARN IT!

Stolen data is only of use if the hacker can understand and exploit the information it contains. Encrypting a file makes it harder to read its contents. It does not, of itself, make it harder to steal the file.

Revision Guide
page 6

LEARN IT!

Collaborative working is when two or more people work together to produce something.

Hint

You should identify how collaborative working can be supported, then give a reason why cloud computing will help achieve this.

LEARN IT!

One type of cloud computing solution involves local devices each running downloaded software to edit files, with an online server storing the files so that multiple users can open them.

(b) The company uses cloud computing technologies to allow staff to work together on designing its greetings cards.

Explain **two** ways that cloud computing can support collaborative working.

1 ....

....

....

....

2 ....

....

....

....

4 marks

(c) The company's data security manager wants to improve the computer system's security from the threat of attack. She has employed an ethical hacker to carry out a penetration test.

Explain **two** benefits to the business of using penetration testing.

1 ....

....

....

....

2 ....

....

....

....

4 marks

Revision Guide
page 32

Hint

First, identify two specific ways that penetration testing can help the business, then for each give a reason how or why it would do this.

Watch out!

The question does not ask for drawbacks to the business.

LEARN IT!

A penetration test is designed to test the strength of a digital system's defences in a controlled and safe way.

Revision Guide
page 52

Hint

Draw questions expect you to produce an annotated diagram showing a process. In this case, you need to include the information contained in the question – the process used to show the cards that meet the search criteria. Make sure you show the information clearly.

Watch out!

Make sure that your annotations show how the data flows through the process. Remember to use the correct shapes and connectors in your diagram. Do not include unnecessary information or detail.

LEARN IT!

A data flow diagram will show how the entities and processes interact to enable information to flow from one part of the system to another.

(d) The company also sells its greetings cards through its website. Customers can use the website to search for different types of greetings card.

Figure 1 shows part of the process the website uses to identify which greetings cards meet the customer's search criteria.

- The customer enters the type of card they are looking for.

- The website checks which cards in the card data store meet the customer's search criteria.

- The card data store gives a list of cards matching the customer's criteria to the website.

- The website shows the customer the list of suitable cards.

Figure 1

On the next page, draw a top-level (Level 0) data flow diagram showing the process the greetings card website uses for showing suitable cards.

Prepare

Think about your diagram before drawing it. You could do a small sketch if it will help you try out your ideas, but don't spend too much time on it. Make sure you cross out any rough work.

LEARN IT!

There are three parts to a Level 0 data flow diagram:

- the system
- the external entities which input and/or output data to or from the system
- the data flows between the entities and the system.

6 marks

Total for Question 3 = 16 marks

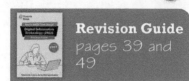

Revision Guide
pages 39 and
49

Watch out!

Make sure you explain a benefit to the retailer. The question does not ask for drawbacks or the impact on website users.

Hint

The retailer is a business. This means it will want to have as many customers as possible spending money on its products.

LEARN IT!

First-party cookies are placed on a user's computer by the website. They include session cookies which are deleted when the user closes their browser. Third-party cookies are placed there by other organisations, such as those that manage the placing of adverts onto the web page. Advertisers are likely to pay more if they know that their advert will be seen by users with an interest in their products.

4　A food and grocery retailer has stores located around the country. It also has a website where customers can view details of products and purchase them online.

(a) The website places a cookie on the computer of each visitor who gives permission for it to do so.

Explain **one** benefit to the retailer of using cookies.

....

....

....

....

2 marks

(b) The website asks visitors to enable it to know their location when they are viewing the website.

Describe how the retailer could use location-based information to provide tailored services to its website customers.

....

....

....

....

....

....

3 marks

(c) An employee wishes to connect their laptop to the internet in order to email a document to a colleague.

Explain **one** way that the employee could use a personal hotspot on their mobile phone to connect the laptop to the internet.

....

....

....

....

....

....

3 marks

Revision Guide
pages 38 and 1

Hint

Describe questions ask you to give two or more linked points. You do not need to include a justification or reason.

LEARN IT!

Location-based services are ones that differ depending on where the user is located.

Hint

Think about the ways that the content of the website could differ depending on where the customer is located.

Hint

This explain question requires you to identify an action the user could take, then justify and expand the answer to show how the laptop could connect to the internet.

Explore

Location-based services only work if the user gives permission for their device to track their location and share this with organisations that request it. Should users be concerned about the privacy issues involved with giving their location to other people and businesses?

LEARN IT!

Make sure you know the difference between a personal hotspot (an ad hoc Wi-Fi network) and tethering (using a wired USB connection).

Hint

A discussion should include well-developed points that link together. For example, you should make a link between how customers might respond and how this impacts on the business.

Prepare

Plan your answer by thinking about the potential impacts and then how the business might be affected by each. This could include the impact on:

* customers
* business operations
* meeting legal requirements.

LEARN IT!

The impact on the retailer will include how many customers it has and the revenue it earns from selling products to them.

(d) The retailer recently suffered a security breach. Some customer data including usernames and passwords was stolen.

Discuss the impact of a security breach on the business.

....

....

....

....

....

....

....

....

....

....

....

....

....

....

....

....

....

....

....

....

....

6 marks

(e) The retailer is considering the following measures to minimise threats to its data.

- Option 1: Locking all doors into rooms containing computer devices.

- Option 2: Facial recognition software to unlock all computer devices.

Evaluate which option would have the greatest impact.

....

....

....

....

....

....

....

....

....

....

....

....

....

....

....

....

....

....

....

....

6 marks

Total for Question 4 = 20 marks

TOTAL FOR ASSESSMENT = 60 MARKS

Revision Guide
pages 27 and 28

Hint

Evaluate questions require you to consider different aspects of a subject, for example, its strengths and weaknesses or advantages and disadvantages. At the end of your answer you should come to an overall judgement about the issue and this should be supported by evidence.

Hint

To evaluate, you need to consider the strengths and weaknesses of each method, then make a judgement as to which method will improve security the most.

Hint

Make sure you give reasons for all your points. For example, why does Option 1 have drawbacks? Why have you chosen one method as being more secure than the other?

Prepare

Briefly plan your answer by making a list of strengths and weaknesses of each option. Then recommend the method you think would be the most suitable ('In conclusion, the best method to use would be... because...').

Revision Guide
page 23

Hint

State questions expect you to recall one or more pieces of information.

Hint

When answering this **state** question, you only need to recall two types of malware. You do not need to go into any detail. Remember only to give the required number of responses.

Hint

When answering this **state** question, you need to recall two **other** methods that can be used to send phishing messages. Phone calls are mentioned in the scenario, so your response should not repeat this as a method.

LEARN IT!

Make sure you know the difference between phishing and pharming. Pharming uses fake websites rather than fake messages to trick the user into giving out information.

Explore

In 2017, over £4.6 billion was stolen from British internet users. Much of this was the result of successful phishing attempts.

Practice assessment 2

> **Answer ALL questions.**
> **Write your answers in the spaces provided.**

1 Jack is a journalist for an online newspaper.
   He works from home and in the newspaper's office.
   Jack's laptop has been attacked by malware.

   (a) State **two** types of malware.

   1 ....

   ....

   2 ....

   ....

   > 2 marks

   (b) Jack knows that phone calls are used to send phishing messages.

   State **two** other methods used to send phishing messages.

   1 ....

   ....

   2 ....

   ....

   > 2 marks

(c) Jack has a visual impairment. He uses accessibility features to help him read information.

Explain **one** accessibility feature Jack can use.

....

....

....

....

2 marks

Revision Guide
pages 17 and 24

Hint

Explain questions require you to support your point with a linked reason.

Hint

In this **explain** question, you need to identify one accessibility feature that could make the information on screen more readable, then show how this will help Jack. Use linking phrases such as '... which means that...' or '... this results in...'.

Watch out!

In 1(c), make sure the feature will help Jack to read information. Do not discuss accessibility features that may help users with other needs.

(d) The newspaper requires all staff to protect themselves from shoulder surfing when working in a public place.

Describe **one** way that Jack could protect the newspaper's data from a shoulder surfer.

....

....

....

....

2 marks

Hint

Describe questions ask you to give two or more linked points that show how something might happen. You do not need to include a justification or reason.

Hint

In this **describe** question, you need to decide on one action that Jack could take and then show how this could protect the information visible on screen.

Watch out!

Make sure that the action you suggest will protect Jack's information from shoulder surfing and not from another form of data theft such as ransomware.

Revision Guide
pages 20 and
21

Hint

In this **explain** question, you need to recall two impacts that technology can have on a user's well-being, then show how the technology can cause this impact.

Hint

Well-being usually means a person's mental or emotional health. However, you could also discuss the impact on their **physical** well-being such as the possible impact on levels of fitness.

Hint

Impacts can be either positive or negative. For example, technology can lead to social interaction or it can be a cause of social isolation.

Watch out!

Make sure your answer explains **two** different impacts on an individual's well-being. The question does not ask you about the impact on the organisation they work for.

(e) The newspaper is concerned about the impact of technology on the well-being of its staff.

Explain **two** impacts of technology on an individual's well-being.

1 ....

....

....

....

2 ....

....

....

....

4 marks

Total for Question 1 = 12 marks

2 A hospital stores confidential patient records. It has safeguards in place to protect this data.

(a) The hospital uses ethical hackers to help protect its systems.

Identify **two** types of ethical hacker.

1 ....

....

2 ....

....

2 marks

(b) The hospital currently replaces its computers every five years.

It is considering replacing its computers every three years.

Explain **one** impact that this change may have on the environment.

....

....

....

....

2 marks

Revision Guide
pages 32, 40
and 41

Hint

Identify questions may ask you to recall a specific piece of information.

Hint

For this **identify** question, you need only name the two types of ethical hacker. You do not need to go into any detail.

Hint

To answer this **explain** question, you need to give an impact of the change on the environment, then say how or why it will have this effect.

 **Prepare**

In 2(b), this policy will mean that the hospital buys new computers more often. It will also mean that its computers are up to date. How will this affect the environment?

Revision Guide
page 63

Hint

Annotate questions require you to label a diagram in the context of the question.

Hint

To **annotate** this form, you need to show a total of **two** ways it could be improved. The improvements should make it easier for users to complete the form.

Watch out!

You only need to state what the improvement is – you don't need to explain the reason for it.

Prepare

Look carefully at the form and identify areas where it isn't user friendly, for example, response boxes that are too small to fit the data. Think about how these parts of the form could be improved.

(c) Hospital reception staff enter a patient's personal details onto a form on their first visit to the hospital.

Annotate the form by:

- identifying and labelling two ways in which the form could be made more user friendly
- stating the improvements that could be made.

An example has been provided.

> Add a heading, to make the purpose of the form clear.

Name

Address

Date of birth

Contact phone number

GP details

4 marks

(d) The hospital has a password policy.

Explain **two** reasons why the hospital has a password policy.

1 ....

....

....

....

2 ....

....

....

....

4 marks

Total for Question 2 = 12 marks

Revision Guide
page 34

Hint

For this **explain** question, you need to provide two reasons why the hospital has a password policy and show how the policy meets this need.

Watch out!

You only need to give **two** reasons.

Prepare

Decide on two features of a password policy. For each feature, think how it helps to increase data security or meets other needs, such as legal requirements.

Watch out!

Make sure you know the main features of a password policy and how this is different from other types of digital usage policies.

Watch out!

Do not write about drawbacks.

Revision Guide
page 2

Hint

For this **explain** question, you should recall one reason for poor mobile network coverage.

Watch out!

Do not give more than **one** reason.

Watch out!

Some reasons for poor network availability will not apply to rural locations.

Hint

People who live in cities will sometimes have poor mobile network availability, but the reasons are likely to be different from those facing rural users.

Explore

In 2018, 9% of the UK did not have good outdoor 4G coverage from any operator. This was mostly in rural areas.

3 Jemma runs a business letting out holiday cottages to guests.

(a) The cottages are in a rural area with poor mobile network coverage.

Explain **one** reason for the poor network availability.

....

....

....

....

2 marks

(b) Jemma's holiday cottages are on social media.

Explain **two** benefits to the business of using social media.

1 ....

....

....

....

2 ....

....

....

....

4 marks

Revision Guide
pages 15 and 16

Hint

To answer this **explain** question, you need to decide on two ways that Jemma's holiday cottages could benefit from using social media, and then say how social media will help to achieve this.

 Prepare

Think about how social media can help Jemma to attract guests to her holiday cottages.

Watch out!

The benefits should refer to the holiday cottage business. Do not discuss drawbacks or Jemma's personal social media use.

Watch out!

Do not give more than **two** benefits.

Revision Guide
page 16

Hint

To answer this **explain** question, you need to develop two reasons why Jemma would wish to use email to communicate with her guests.

Prepare

Think about why Jemma might wish to communicate with her current and future guests.

Watch out!

Make sure your answer covers why Jemma would wish to communicate with her guests. The question is **not** asking you to consider why guests would wish to be emailed or why they might wish to email Jemma.

Watch out!

Do not give more than **two** reasons.

(c) Jemma requests that guests supply an email address when they book one of her cottages. This allows her to send an email confirmation of their booking.

Explain **two** other reasons why Jemma may wish to collect guests' email addresses.

1 ....

....

....

....

2 ....

....

....

....

4 marks

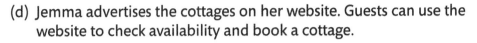

(d) Jemma advertises the cottages on her website. Guests can use the website to check availability and book a cottage.

Figure 1 shows part of the process the website uses to identify what cottages are available on a guest's preferred dates.

- The guest enters the date(s) for their stay.
- The website checks which cottage is available in the cottage data store.
- The cottage data store gives a list of available cottages to the website.
- The website shows the guest a list of available cottages.

Figure 1

On the next page, draw a top-level (Level 0) data flow diagram to show the process the holiday cottages website uses for showing availability.

Hint

Draw questions expect you to produce an annotated diagram showing a process. In this case, you need to include the information contained in Figure 1, the process used to show availability of cottages on a given date. Make sure you show the information clearly.

Watch out!

Make sure that your annotations show how the data flows through the process. Remember to use the correct shapes and connectors in your diagram. Do not include unnecessary information or detail.

LEARN IT!

A data flow diagram will show how the entities and processes interact to enable information to flow from one part of a system to another.

Prepare

Think about your diagram before drawing it. You could do a small sketch if it will help you try out your ideas, but don't spend too much time on it. Make sure you cross out any rough work.

LEARN IT!

There are three parts to a
Level 0 data flow diagram:

1 the system

2 the external entities
which input and/or
output data to or from
the system

3 the data flows between
the entities and the
system.

6 marks

Total for Question 3 = 16 marks

4 An online magazine employs writers who live in different countries around the world.

(a) All the writers are given the same level of access to the magazine's digital systems.

Describe **one** way levels of permitted access can improve system security.

....

....

....

....

2 marks

Revision Guide
page 28

Hint

In this **describe** question, you need to provide two points that together show how levels of access help increase system security.

Hint

Remember you don't need to include an explanation of why the system security needs improving.

Watch out!

Make sure you know the difference between levels of permitted access (sometimes called access rights) and user accessibility needs.

LEARN IT!

Levels of access can help to limit a user's access to data and software on a network, access to data on a cloud storage account and read-only or full editing rights to shared data.

Revision Guide
pages 41 and 2

Hint

In this **explain** question, you need to give three connected points which together show how the impact on the environment can be reduced by the use of power-saving settings.

Hint

This is an **explain** question, so you need to show you understand how using power-saving settings results in benefits to the environment.

LEARN IT!

Energy-saving features include:
- auto power-off
- power-saving mode
- sleep mode.

LEARN IT!

An open Wi-Fi network transmits data in unencrypted plain text, so any data sent using the network could be read by anyone connected to it.

Prepare

In Question 4(c), think of a problem that could result from a document being intercepted by an unauthorised user. Then expand your point by exploring how this could affect the magazine business. Use words such as 'so' or 'which' to help you do this.

(b) The magazine aims to reduce its impact on the environment. It uses power-saving settings on all devices.

Explain how the use of power-saving settings reduces the magazine's impact on the environment.

....

....

....

....

....

....

3 marks

(c) A writer is planning to connect their laptop to an open Wi-Fi network so they can email a document to a colleague.

Explain **one** drawback to the magazine of using an open Wi-Fi network to send documents.

....

....

....

....

....

....

3 marks

(d) The magazine's writers collaborate to produce articles.

Discuss how writers in different countries can make effective use of online collaboration tools.

....

....

....

....

....

....

....

....

....

....

....

....

....

....

....

....

....

....

....

....

....

6 marks

Revision Guide
pages 6 and 13

Hint

Discuss questions expect you to identify an issue, situation or problem that is referred to in the question, and then explore different aspects of it.

Hint

For this **discuss** question, use your knowledge of collaboration tools to show how they could be used by writers to produce better articles.

Watch out!

Do **not** explain how collaboration tools work or how they impact on the magazine.

Hint

Explore points in depth, for example, by identifying tools, then showing how they could be used by writers to collaborate. Then explore what the writers would need to do in order to use the tools well.

Prepare

Plan your discussion. For example:

- Identify collaboration tools.

- Explain how each tool can be used to help writers collaborate with each other.

- Discuss any potential issues to be overcome, such as writers operating in different countries and time zones.

Revision Guide
page 5

Hint

Evaluate means that you need to consider the strengths and weaknesses (or advantages and disadvantages) and come to a justified conclusion as to which option you think is the best for the magazine. This means you need to give a reason for your conclusion.

Prepare

Make a brief plan of your answer. For example:

- Identify the benefits and drawbacks for the magazine of each proposal.
- Which option is best for the magazine? What are the main reasons for recommending this option?

Watch out!

Make sure you know the difference between online applications and cloud storage.

Watch out!

Do not discuss how the two proposals would work. Focus instead on the impact of each technology.

Hint

Make sure any examples you include are related to the context of the question/scenario, in this case the magazine and its writers.

(e) The magazine is considering two proposals to improve their use of cloud computing:

Proposal 1: Use online applications

Proposal 2: Use cloud storage.

Evaluate which proposal would have the most impact on the magazine.

....

....

....

....

....

....

....

....

....

....

....

....

....

....

....

....

....

....

6 marks

Total for Question 4 = 20 marks

TOTAL FOR ASSESSMENT = 60 MARKS

Practice assessment 3

Revision Guide
pages 4, 5
and 10

> **Answer ALL questions.**
> **Write your answers in the spaces provided.**

1 An engineering company designs and builds boats.

(a) The company uses cloud storage for its data.

Give **two** benefits to the company of using cloud storage.

1 ....

....

2 ....

....

`2 marks`

(b) The company is looking for a cloud services provider that has a disaster recovery policy.

State **two** other factors the company should consider when choosing a cloud services provider.

1 ....

....

2 ....

....

`2 marks`

Hint

Give questions expect you to provide one or more features of a situation.

Hint

When you **give** a benefit, you need to provide a single statement. For example, a benefit of data encryption is 'It makes it harder for hackers to gain access to information.' You do not need to develop your answer.

Hint

For this **state** question, think about **two** cloud services the company may need and then write a statement about each.

LEARN IT!

Cloud storage providers offer a single service of file storage and synchronisation. Cloud computing providers offer a range of services, including tools for collaboration and applications accessed from a web browser.

Watch out!

Avoid using disaster recovery in your answer as this is already covered.

Revision Guide
pages 21 and 23

Hint

When you **give** two drawbacks, you should show **two** different ways that the employees' well-being may be affected. There is no need to develop your answer.

Watch out!

Make sure you give drawbacks to employees that result from having work phones switched on outside work. You are not asked to consider the impact on the company. Only give the required number of responses.

Hint

Explain questions require you to support your point with a linked reason.

Hint

When you answer this **explain** question, you should recall one way the company could reduce the threat from ransomware, then show how the method would achieve this.

Watch out!

You're not required to explain what ransomware is or how your chosen method works. Instead, focus on how the method will help to prevent this type of malware from attacking the company's devices.

(c) The engineering company provides mobile phones to some of its employees. The phones must be left switched on when the employees are out of the office.

Give **two** drawbacks to employees of using mobile phones in this way.

1 ....

....

2 ....

....

2 marks

(d) The company has recently been the victim of a ransomware attack.

Explain **one** way that the company could protect itself against ransomware.

....

....

....

....

2 marks

(e) The company has introduced an environmental policy.

Explain **two** ways the policy could help the company to reduce the impact of its digital systems on the environment.

1 ....

....

....

....

2 ....

....

....

....

4 marks

Total for Question 1 = 12 marks

Revision Guide
pages 40 and 41

Hint

When you **explain**, you should recall two actions the company could take, then for each action give a reason how or why the impact on the environment will improve.

Watch out!

Make sure you only cover **two** actions. Each action needs to be developed. It is not enough simply to state the action. Each action must have a positive impact on the environment.

LEARN IT!

Computers need electricity to function. This can be supplied by battery or direct from the mains. Devices contain components made using non-renewable materials such as lithium, nickel, copper, gold and silver.

Explore

The Waste Electrical and Electronic Equipment (WEEE) Regulations were introduced to encourage the recovery, reuse and recycling of electrical and electronic equipment.

Revision Guide
pages 49 and 50

Hint

When you answer this **give** question, you need to recall **two** ways that using cookies can benefit the owner of a website.

LEARN IT!

Session cookies are used by the owner of a website to store information about a visitor's use of the website. The information contained is often deleted when the browser is closed. Third-party cookies are used by organisations that provide advertising on the website. They record information about browsing history to provide adverts that are relevant to the user.

Hint

For this **explain** question, you need to think of **one** action the copyright holder could take, then develop it, for example, by showing how the leisure centre could be affected by the action.

LEARN IT!

A copyright holder owns the right to decide when and how an original product can be used. They are not always the person who created the product.

2 A leisure centre has a website where members can book fitness classes.

(a) The leisure centre uses cookies to store data when members visit the website.

Give **two** ways that the leisure centre could benefit from using cookies in this way.

....

....

....

....

2 marks

(b) The leisure centre has used an image on its website without seeking permission from the copyright holder.

Explain **one** action the copyright holder could take against the fitness centre.

....

....

....

....

2 marks

(c) New members can apply to join the leisure centre online. They complete a form with their details.

Annotate the form by:

- identifying and labelling where two different data protection principles are not being applied

- stating how each data protection principle is not being applied.

An example has been provided.

4 marks

Leisure centre member information

Please enter the following personal information:

Name:

Address:

Mobile number:

Email address:

Social media account(s):

Annual income:

Please note: We will store this information for five years. ← Storing information: This period is too long. Information should be stored only for as long as is necessary.

Please note: We may use this information for other purposes.

Hint

Annotate questions require you to label a diagram and provide an explanation for each feature you identify.

Hint

To answer this **annotate** question, you need to show how any **two** parts of the form do not meet data protection principles.

Watch out!

Do not give more than the required number of responses.

Prepare

Study each part of the form. Decide what, if any, data protection principles have not been met. Then, for each, think of a reason how or why the principle is not being followed.

LEARN IT!

The requirements to protect personal information were first set out in the Data Protection Act 1998. These were updated in the Data Protection Act 2018, which implemented the General Data Protection Regulation (GDPR).

Hint

To answer this **explain** question, think of **two** reasons why the leisure centre would use a private communication channel. You could then develop your answer by giving an example of a suitable type of message.

Watch out!

Remember to focus your answer in the context of a leisure centre. For example, you could consider the types of messages that a leisure centre would send using a private communication channel.

LEARN IT!

Check you know the difference between private and public communication channels and which types of information could be sent using each method.

(d) The leisure centre often sends messages to members using private communication channels such as email.

Explain **two** reasons why the leisure centre would use private communication channels.

1 ....

....

....

....

2 ....

....

....

....

4 marks

Total for Question 2 = 12 marks

3 A medical centre stores confidential information about patients and their treatments.

(a) The medical centre secures its digital systems using different levels of permitted access.

Explain **one** other method the medical centre could use to restrict access to patient information.

....

....

....

....

2 marks

Hint

To answer this **explain** question, you need to recall one method of user access restriction, then demonstrate how it could help to prevent unauthorised access to a digital system.

Watch out!

Avoid writing about how organisations set different levels of access for authorised users. You are asked for another method of keeping a system secure. Remember to give only the required number of responses.

LEARN IT!

Levels of permitted access prevent authorised users of a system from gaining access to specific areas, for example, denying them access to certain files or programs.

Revision Guide
page 37

Hint

To answer this **explain** question, you need to recall two actions an organisation should take following a cyberattack, then demonstrate how each action could help the medical centre to return quickly to normal working.

Watch out!

Focus your answer on what the centre should do following an attack. Do not explain the reasons for and the contents of a disaster recovery policy.

Explore

In 2017, the National Health Service (NHS) was a victim of a ransomware attack called WannaCry. The cost to the NHS was over £90 million. In 2018, an NHS report identified some of the lessons learned as a result of the attack.

LEARN IT!

Make sure you know that the actions to be taken following a cyberattack are one part of a disaster recovery policy.

(b) The medical centre has a disaster recovery plan to recover its digital systems if they are attacked.

Explain **two** actions that the medical centre should take following a cyberattack.

1 ....

....

....

....

2 ....

....

....

....

4 marks

(c) The medical centre allows patients to book appointments either in person at the centre or by using a smartphone app. The appointments app is only available for one type of smartphone operating system.

Explain **two** reasons why the medical centre is failing to provide equal access to all its patients.

1 ....

....

....

....

2 ....

....

....

....

4 marks

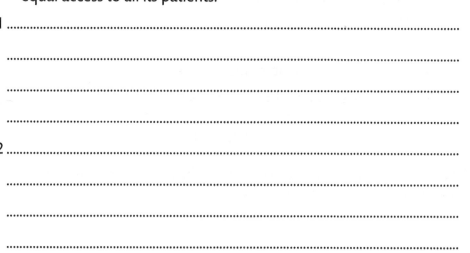

Revision Guide
page 42

Hint

In this **explain** question, you need to give **two** reasons, then for each show how or why they result in some users not having access to the medical centre's services.

Watch out!

The question asks you to explain two reasons, so make sure you do not just repeat the question.

Prepare

Make sure you understand how users can access the existing service. Think about why the example given might mean that some users do not have access to the service. Then think of one other possible reason.

Revision Guide
page 53

Hint

Draw questions may expect you to produce a flow chart showing a process.

Hint

When answering this **draw** question, you need to construct a flow chart that includes all the steps in Figure 1.

Hint

Use the correct flow chart symbols for each action in Figure 1. Show the sequence in which each action takes place. Some actions might depend on the outcome of a previous decision.

Draw a rough sketch of your diagram first. Check you have used the correct shapes and linked the actions together in the correct way.

Watch out!

All flow charts include some actions that are not included in Figure 1. Make sure you include these in your diagram.

(d) The smartphone app allows patients to book an appointment within the next five days.

Figure 1 shows part of the process the app uses to offer an appointment.

> • Ask patient for preferred date.
> • Check whether the patient's preferred date is within the next five days.
> • If yes, offer an available slot.
> • If no, advise patient to try again later.

Figure 1

Draw a flow chart to show the processes the app uses to offer an appointment within the next five days.

6 marks

Total for Question 3 = 16 marks

4 A theme park uses digital systems to help manage its services to customers.

(a) The theme park uses penetration testing to identify weaknesses in its digital systems.

Describe **one** way the theme park could use penetration testing to improve its digital security.

....

....

....

....

2 marks

Practice assessment

③

Revision Guide
page 32

Hint

For this **describe** question, you need to recall relevant features of penetration testing and link them together to show how the theme park could use this method to improve its security. You don't need to give reasons why the theme park uses penetration testing.

Watch out!

You do not need to describe how penetration testing works. Use your knowledge of how it could be used.

Explore

An organisation wishing to improve its security may ask an ethical hacker to do the penetration test.

LEARN IT!

A penetration test has five main stages:

1. agreeing requirements
2. researching publicly available information about the organisation
3. carrying out penetration tests
4. collecting and analysing the results
5. reporting back with recommendations.

Hint

For this **explain** question, you need to give a benefit of using web-based software, explain why this is and then expand your point by showing how this will benefit the theme park. Use connective words such as 'because' to help you do this.

LEARN IT!

Web-based software is stored on a remote server and accessed using a web browser connected to the internet.

Watch out!

In 4(b), make sure that you focus on a benefit to the theme park business and not its employees or its customers.

Watch out!

In 4(c), make sure you give an account of how the attacker's actions could result in the theft of data.

Explore

Most 'man-in-the-middle' attacks can be prevented by encrypting the data being exchanged, as this makes it unlikely that any intercepted data could be used by the attacker.

(b) The theme park uses a cloud computing service. The service includes word-processing and spreadsheet software that can be accessed over the internet using a web browser.

Explain **one** way that using web-based software can benefit the theme park.

....

....

....

....

....

....

3 marks

(c) An employee replies to an email message from a colleague while connected to an open Wi-Fi network. The message contains confidential information. The information is captured by a 'man-in-the-middle' attacker.

Explain how a 'man-in-the-middle' attacker could steal data.

....

....

....

....

....

....

3 marks

(d) The theme park is an inclusive place to work. It uses technology to ensure its workplace has employees with the skills and talents it needs.

Discuss how technologies can help to make a workplace more inclusive.

....

....

....

....

....

....

....

....

....

....

....

....

....

....

....

....

....

....

....

....

....

....

....

6 marks

Revision Guide
page 20

Hint

Discuss questions expect you to consider in detail the different aspects of an issue, situation, problem or argument and how they interrelate.

Prepare

Think about what inclusivity means. Then consider how technology can help an organisation to have access to the best possible workforce. Make sure your discussion links to the context of the question.

Prepare

Produce a brief plan of your answer. For example:

- State what is meant by 'an inclusive workplace'.
- Identify technologies that could help make a workplace inclusive.
- Explain how each technology could make the workplace inclusive.
- Discuss any problems the technologies might bring.

Watch out!

Make sure your discussion covers more than assistive technology. Inclusivity includes how the use of technologies can support people with specific needs.

Revision Guide
pages 30 and 31

Hint

This **evaluate** question requires you to consider the impact that these two proposals would have on the digital security of the theme park. You need to decide which proposal would have the biggest impact and give reasons for your conclusion.

Hint

You do not need to explain how each proposal would work.

Prepare

Produce a brief plan of your answer. For example:
- State what is meant by anti-virus and firewall software, and data encryption.
- Identify and then discuss benefits of using each technology.
- Conclusion: Which method would have the biggest impact? Say why you have chosen this method.

(e) The theme park is considering two proposals to improve its digital security.

- Proposal 1: Install anti-virus and firewall software on all devices.
- Proposal 2: Encrypt all data stored on its devices.

Evaluate which proposal would have the most positive impact on the theme park.

....

....

....

....

....

....

....

....

....

....

....

....

....

....

....

....

....

....

....

....

....

6 marks

Total for Question 4 = 20 marks

TOTAL FOR ASSESSMENT = 60 MARKS

Practice assessment 4

Revision Guide
pages 14, 45
and 46

> **Answer ALL questions.**
> **Write your answers in the spaces provided.**

1 A firm of architects designs houses and office buildings.

(a) The firm uses project planning software.

Identify **two** features of project planning software.

Tick the boxes.

☐ Assign tasks to individuals

☐ Customise animations

☐ Invite colleagues to a meeting

☐ Send email messages

☐ Set deadlines for tasks

`2 marks`

(b) The firm has an acceptable use policy.

Describe **one** feature of an acceptable use policy.

....

....

....

....

`2 marks`

Time it!

Question 1 carries 12 out of the 60 marks for the paper. You should aim to spend 15–20 minutes answering it.

Hint

Identify questions may ask you to select key information from a list or source.

Hint

In 1(a), if you are not sure of **two** correct responses, try to identify any items that are not features of the software. This may help you to work out the right answers.

Hint

For this **describe** question, you should recall one feature of an acceptable use policy, then develop your response, for example by saying what this part of the policy might contain. You do not need to include a reason why the policy is used.

Watch out!

Make sure you know the difference between an acceptable use policy and a password policy or software policy. Do not give features of these other policies.

Revision Guide
pages 34 and 3

Hint

To answer this **explain** question, you need to recall one feature of a strong password, then develop your answer by demonstrating how the feature helps to make the password hard to guess.

Explore

Strong passwords are often hard to remember. Alternatives to passwords, such as biometrics, are likely to be increasingly used in the future.

Watch out!

In 1(d), do not write about how cloud storage works. Use your knowledge to explain how the firm benefits from using it.

Watch out!

There are many ways in which using cloud storage can benefit an organisation. Make sure your answer focuses on data security.

(c) The firm has a password policy. The policy requires users to create a strong password.

Explain **one** feature of a strong password.

....

....

....

....

2 marks

(d) The firm uses cloud storage providers. Copies of its data are stored on several different servers.

Explain **one** way that storing data on several servers can help to keep it secure.

....

....

....

....

2 marks

(e) An architect connects to an open Wi-Fi network whilst on a train.

Explain **two** ways that an open Wi-Fi network may not be secure.

1 ....

....

....

....

2 ....

....

....

....

4 marks

Total for Question 1 = 12 marks

Revision Guide
page 2

Hint

When responding to this **explain** question, recall two security problems caused by using open networks, then show how they may put data at risk.

Prepare

Think about the security weaknesses of an open network. How easy is it to set up a network? Are passwords needed to connect to it? How is data transmitted across the network?

Explore

Websites that exchange data using https are more secure than those using http. Some browsers display a warning when a user tries to connect to a website that uses http. This helps to make open Wi-Fi networks safer to use.

Revision Guide
pages 17 and
45

Time it!

Question 2 carries 12 out of the 60 marks for the paper. You should aim to spend 15–20 minutes answering it.

Hint

For 2(a), you should give **one** way that alt text could be used, then show how this would help people with a visual impairment.

Hint

There are only two marks for Question 2(a). This is a clue that you only need to explain one way.

Watch out!

In 2(a), you don't need to explain what alt text is or identify the needs of users. Do not give more than **one** way that alt text could help.

Hint

For Question 2(b), you should give two linked points that together show how the streaming service will be affected by the employee's actions.

Watch out!

Avoid discussing the impact on the employee or other policies covering acceptable use in Question (b).

2 An online streaming service supplies music to its customers through a website and apps.

(a) The website uses alt text.

Explain how alt text could help users with visual impairment to use the site.

....

....

....

....

2 marks

(b) The streaming service's acceptable use policy states that staff must not use social media to post negative comments about their work.

Explain **one** impact on the business of an employee posting negative comments on social media.

....

....

....

....

2 marks

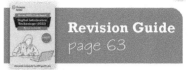
(c) The streaming service has produced a form to allow customers to search for music.

Annotate the form by:

- identifying and labelling two different improvements that could be made to make it more user friendly

- stating how each feature makes it more user friendly.

An example has been provided.

4 marks

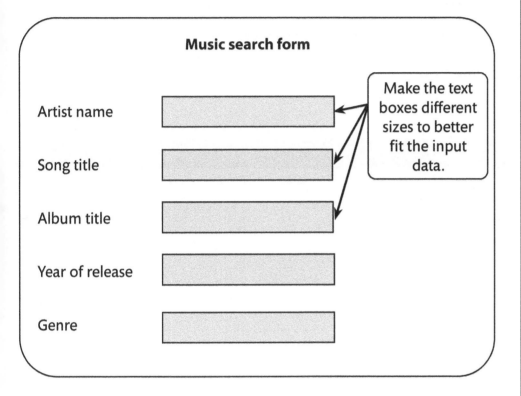

Music search form

Artist name

Song title

Album title

Year of release

Genre

Make the text boxes different sizes to better fit the input data.

Hint

Annotate questions require you to label a diagram. Here you also need to state how each feature makes it more user friendly.

Hint

To **annotate** the form, you should draw an arrow to each part that could be improved. Then write one improvement linked to each arrow.

Hint

You could either suggest improvements to items already on the form or suggest things that could be added to the form. Some improvements could benefit all users, while others may benefit users with specific needs.

Prepare

Think of the main features of a form that could aid accessibility. Which ones would improve this form? Make rough notes before you annotate the diagram.

Revision Guide
page 44

Hint

To answer this **explain** question, you should recall two benefits of net neutrality for providers of online services, then for each give a reason why they benefit in this way.

LEARN IT!

Net neutrality does not cover the quality of service that ISPs offer to their customers, so, for example, they can charge more for faster download speeds. Net neutrality prevents the ISP treating data differently depending on which online business is supplying it.

Watch out!

Do not write about drawbacks or the impact on others such as customers.

Explore

In the UK, Ofcom, the regulator for communications services, is responsible for monitoring and enforcing open internet access (Open Internet Regulation). Open internet access exists only where legislation protects it.

(d) The streaming service relies on internet service providers (ISPs) following net neutrality rules.

Explain **two** benefits to the streaming service of net neutrality.

1 ....

....

....

....

2 ....

....

....

....

4 marks

Total for Question 2 = 12 marks

3 A clothing manufacturer designs and makes sportswear which it sells online and through high street stores.

(a) One of the company's workers accidentally causes a security breach that results in a loss of data.

Explain how an employee could put the security of the company's data at risk.

....

....

....

....

2 marks

Time it!

Question 3 carries 16 out of the 60 marks for the paper. You should aim to spend 20–25 minutes answering it.

Hint

To answer this **explain** question, you need to recall one way that an internal user could make the system vulnerable, then give a reason why this action would result in data loss.

Hint

Use your knowledge of internal threats to show how they could result in a loss of data. You don't need to explain how internal threats work.

Watch out!

Don't write about threats caused by external hackers, but remember that some internal threats make it easier for hackers to gain access to systems.

Explore

In 2016, researchers deliberately dropped nearly 300 USB storage devices in a university car park. 48% of the devices were picked up, plugged into computers and had their files opened. It only took six minutes for the first device to be used!

Revision Guide
page 27

Hint

To answer this **explain** question, you should recall two software security methods, then give a linked reason why the system will be protected. Do not give more than the required number of responses.

Hint

You do not need to explain in detail how the two software methods work. Use your knowledge of them to give reasons how or why they will help protect the system from security threats.

Watch out!

Avoid explaining encryption software, as this is mentioned in the question.

LEARN IT!

Make sure you know which security measures use software to operate and which ones use physical measures (such as doors locked with a key).

(b) The company protects its digital systems using encryption software.

Explain **two** other software tools that the company could use to protect its systems.

1 ....

....

....

....

2 ....

....

....

....

4 marks

(c) Visitors to the website are asked to share their location. The company aims to meet legal requirements when using this personal information.

Explain **two** legal requirements that the company must comply with when using personal information in this way.

1 ....

....

....

....

2 ....

....

....

....

4 marks

Revision Guide
pages 38 and 39

Hint

To answer this **explain** question, you should recall two legal requirements for the business, then for each give a reason how or why the business is affected by the requirement.

Watch out!

Make sure your answer covers legal requirements. This includes anything that is covered by an Act of Parliament.

LEARN IT!

Websites on smartphones use the phone's location. Smartphones use GPS or the nearest mobile signal mast to work out their location. This data can be shared with a desktop PC if both are connected to the same LAN (local area network).

Revision Guide
page 53

Hint

Draw questions may expect you to produce a data flow diagram or flow chart showing how information moves around in a system.

Hint

When answering **draw** questions, you need to construct a flow chart that includes all the steps in the question.

(d) When customers buy items online for the first time, they are required to create a username and password.

Figure 1 shows the process.

- The customer is asked to enter a username first.

- The system checks whether the username already exists.

- If the username already exists, the customer is asked to enter a different username.

- Customers are not allowed to enter a password until they have entered a unique username.

- The password must be at least eight characters long and contain at least one number and one letter.

- The username and password are not saved until a valid password is entered.

Figure 1

On the next page, draw a flow chart to show the process for when a customer creates a username and password.

Hint

Use the correct flow chart symbols for each action in the question. Show the sequence in which each action takes place. Some actions might depend on the outcome of a previous decision.

 Prepare

Draw a rough sketch of your diagram first. Check you have used the correct shapes and linked the actions together in the correct way.

Watch out!

All flow charts include some actions that are not included in the question. Make sure that you include these in your diagram.

6 marks

Total for Question 3 = 16 marks

Revision Guide
page 27

⏱ Time it!

Question 4 carries 20 out of the 60 marks for the paper. You should aim to spend 25–30 minutes answering it.

Hint

In this **explain** question, you need to include some detail, rather than simply state a fact. Recall one drawback of using password protection, then give a reason **how** or **why** it might affect the company.

Hint

You do not need to explain how password protection works. Use your knowledge to show how its use could harm the company.

Watch out!

Make sure the drawback is relevant to how passwords restrict access to digital systems. Do not give a benefit.

---

4 A software development company creates apps for its clients.

(a) The company uses passwords to protect its digital systems.

Explain **one** drawback of using passwords to protect the company's digital systems from external threats.

....

....

....

....

2 marks

(b) Tanya is a software engineer for the company.

She ensures that all the files she sends to clients are encrypted.

Explain how data encryption improves data security.

....

....

....

....

....

....

3 marks

(c) Tanya sometimes creates documents while working in the office, which she then edits when working at home.

Explain **one** benefit to the business of using cloud computing to synchronise these files across devices.

....

....

....

....

....

3 marks

Hint

In this **explain** question, give three linked statements that together show how encrypting data helps to keep it secure.

Watch out!

You do not need to explain how data encryption works.

Prepare

In Question 4(b), think about how data is encrypted and what needs to happen to enable the contents of the file to be read by the client. How does this help to keep the data secure from anyone else who tries to view it?

LEARN IT!

Cloud computing uses the internet to deliver the data that users need to work with. For example, a copy of a document, which is stored on a remote server, can be downloaded to whichever device Tanya uses to edit it. The edited version is then sent back to the remote server.

Watch out!

In Question 4(c), make sure that you focus on a benefit to the business and not to its employees or customers.

Revision Guide
page 36

(d) A fire at the company's offices has damaged its digital systems.

The company has used its disaster recovery policy to reduce the impact of the fire.

Discuss how a disaster recovery policy can help the company to return to normal working quickly.

....

....

....

....

....

....

....

....

....

....

....

....

....

....

....

....

....

....

....

....

6 marks

(e) The software development company is considering using one of the following two options to replace its existing word-processing software:

- Option 1: Traditional installation (the software is purchased, downloaded and installed onto each individual computer).

- Option 2: Cloud service provider (a monthly fee is paid and the software is accessed using a web browser).

Evaluate which option would have the most positive impact on the software development company.

....

....

....

....

....

....

....

....

....

....

....

....

....

....

....

....

6 marks

Total for Question 4 = 20 marks

TOTAL FOR ASSESSMENT = 60 MARKS

Revision Guide
page 9

Hint

In this **evaluate** question, you need to discuss the strengths (benefits) and weaknesses (drawbacks) of each of the two options before making a recommendation as to which option the company should choose. Give reasons to explain your recommendations.

Prepare

Identify the benefits and drawbacks of each option. These could include the impact on money spent, system requirements or work produced using the software. Develop your ideas by linking together points to explain each impact in detail.

Prepare

Think about how the reasons for your recommendation relate to the strengths and weaknesses of the two options. For example, you should only recommend Option 1 if you can explain why it is better than Option 2.

Time it!

Work out how long you have spent answering Question 4 so far. If you have stuck to the time plan, you should have about 10 minutes left for 4(e). Spend no more than two minutes on your plan, then about three minutes discussing each option, with the final two minutes on your conclusion.

Time it!

If there is time at the end, read through your answer and try to improve it.

Answers

Use this section to check your answers.

- For questions with clear correct answers, these are provided. If there are alternative correct answers, these are given.
- For questions where answers may be individual or require longer answers, bullet points are provided to indicate key points you could include in your answer, or how your answer could be structured. **Your answer should be written using sentences and paragraphs**, and might include some of these points but not necessarily all of them.

> The questions and sample answers are provided to help you revise content and skills. Ask your tutor or check the Pearson website for the most up-to-date Sample Assessment Material, past papers and mark schemes to get an indication of the actual assessment and what this requires of you. Details of the actual assessment may change so always make sure you are up to date.

Practice assessment 1

1 (a) Acceptable responses. Any **two** of the following, for example:
- for fun *or* as a challenge
- industrial espionage/spying
- financial gain
- personal motives
- to cause disruption
- to steal and use data/information.

(b) Individual response. Any **one** of the following, for example:

Anti-virus software:
- acts as a second line of defence, in case employees accidentally download or open a suspicious file
- can monitor all files for signs of suspicious activity, so that the systems can be protected against new, as yet unknown, viruses
- can stop/quarantine/delete malware before it is able to run and infect the system.

(c) Acceptable responses:
- door locks
- swipe card.

(d) Individual responses. Any **one** of the following, for example:

Strengthening passwords:
- by not using a recognisable word, since these can be easily guessed
- by using numbers and special characters that would not form part of a word or phrase
- by using a longer password – longer passwords contain more characters so are harder to guess.

(e) Individual responses, for example:

Changing passwords:
- reduces the chances of their account being hacked since, even though a hacker may obtain the user's password, it is likely to have been changed before they can use it to gain access to the account
- makes the system more secure, by limiting the impact of an out-of-date password being discovered.

2 (a) Acceptable responses. Any **two** of the following, for example:

Data:
- may only be used for specified, explicit purposes
- must be used in a way that is adequate, relevant and limited to only what is necessary
- must be handled in a way that ensures appropriate security, including protection against unlawful or unauthorised processing, access, loss, destruction or damage.

(b) Individual responses. Any **one** of the following, for example:

The employee:
- should use an anti-virus program to scan the attachment for malware. The attachment can be opened if it is safe, otherwise the email/attachment should be deleted
- should not download or open the file but instead scan it for viruses
- may delete the email if they do not trust the sender – this will also delete the attachment.

(c) Your response to this question should identify two accessibility features on the web page with an explanation linked to each feature.

Individual responses. Any **two** of the following, for example:
- a magnifier (add label to magnifiying glass); a magnifier makes the web page easier to view by enlarging sections of the screen
- a narrator (add label to microphone); a narrator (text to speech) reads text on the screen aloud so that users with limited vision can hear the page content
- alt text (add label to image of clothes); alt text describes the content of images for users with limited vision.

(d) Individual responses. Any **two** of the following, for example:

Acceptable software policy:
- ensures only permitted software is installed on the network
- reduces the likelihood of unlicensed copies of software being installed, which may result in the organisation having to pay for licences if discovered
- reduces the potential for users to install software containing malware which could damage digital systems
- ensures that workers can only use the digital system for work purposes, resulting in more work being done
- ensures only approved software is installed, helping to ensure storage capacity isn't exceeded
- ensures only software that is needed is purchased, saving the retailer money
- unauthorised software may contain bugs/be incompatible with the operating system, resulting in resources being used to resolve faults.

3 (a) Individual response. Any **one** of the following, for example:

Data encryption:
- Data is scrambled so anyone viewing the files is unable to understand the information contained.
- Encryption reduces the chances of data theft because the data is unreadable to anyone unable to decrypt it.
- The data is scrambled using an encryption key and can only be accessed by someone who has the key to unscramble it.

(b) Individual responses. Any **two** of the following, for example:

Cloud computing:
- Collaboration tools can be used so that one person can review the work of another.
- Real-time co-authoring is enabled so that two or more people can work together to jointly produce a document.

- Changes made by one user on one device are synchronised so the user on a different device accesses the most up-to-date version.
- Version control is maintained because each user can work on the same document, avoiding the creation of multiple versions.
- Authors are able to share files without needing to email copies to each other.

(c) Individual responses. Any **two** of the following, for example:

Penetration testing:
- can identify weaknesses in system security without causing any harm to systems or data because the aim is not to cause damage
- does not disrupt business operations because the penetration test can be carried out at a non-critical time
- can help to improve system security because the tests will reveal weaknesses and how to overcome them
- can help the business to meet legal requirements for data protection, resulting in less chance of a damaging loss of personal data
- uses the same methods as a malicious attacker would use, so is a realistic test of the system's defences.

(d) Example data flow diagram:

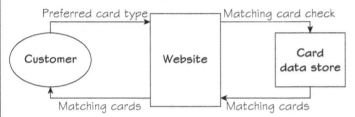

Solutions might use other relevant phrasing/wording in a data flow diagram. The data flow diagram must use correct logic and should produce the expected outcome.

4 (a) Individual response. Any **one** of the following, for example:

Cookies:
- First-party cookies can be used to remember user preferences. This means that the user can be shown information that is more relevant to them, making it more likely they will want to shop there.
- First-party cookies can keep the user logged onto the website so that they can be shown content that makes them more likely to buy items.
- First-party cookies can remember the content of a user's shopping basket so that the user can complete a purchase when they return to the website.
- Third-party cookies can be used to track online activity. This can help the website display content that reflects the user's browsing interests. This makes it more likely that the user will spend more time on the website.

(b) Individual responses. Your description could include any **three** of the following, for example:

Location-based information:
- The device's location can be detected using GPS/local mobile phone masts/nearby Wi-Fi networks.
- This location is shared with the website.
- The website can provide content specific to that location.
- The website could show details of the nearest shops.
- It could only show information about products available in the local shop.

- It could set the text language to that typically used at the local location.
- It could provide videos in the local language(s) typically used at the location.

(c) Individual responses. Any **one** of the following, for example:
- the mobile phone is connected to the internet; the mobile phone also creates an ad hoc Wi-Fi network (hotspot); so the laptop connects to the ad hoc network/hotspot via the mobile phone
- the laptop uses Wi-Fi to connect to the mobile phone; so the data is sent from the laptop to the internet; using the mobile phone's mobile data connection
- the mobile phone uses a mobile signal to connect to the internet; the mobile phone uses a hotspot to connect to the laptop; so the laptop uses the mobile phone's internet connection to send documents via the internet.

(d) Individual response. Your answer should show accurate and detailed knowledge and understanding. Your points should be relevant to the context in the question, with clear links. Your discussion should be well developed and logical, clearly considering different aspects and how they interrelate.

Your discussion may include some of the following points, for example:

The retailer:
- may suffer loss of reputation leading to a loss of customers
- may lose customers, leading to fewer sales and less income
- may have to increase security measures, which may be expensive
- may face prosecution under data protection legislation and may have to pay a fine
- may have to compensate customers who have been victims of identify fraud as a result of the data theft.

(e) Individual response. Your answer should show accurate, detailed knowledge and understanding. Your points should be relevant to the context in the question, with clear links. Your evaluation should be well developed and logical, clearly considering different aspects and competing points in detail, leading to a conclusion that is fully supported.

Your evaluation may include some of the following points, for example:
- Identified possible strengths of Option 1:
  - only people with keys or swipe cards can unlock doors to gain access
  - unauthorised users can be prevented from gaining access to a server room
  - helps to reduce the chances of shoulder surfing.
- Identified possible weaknesses of Option 1:
  - relies on all users unlocking and locking doors
  - doors may be left unlocked, giving access to unauthorised staff or visitors
  - once inside a server room there may be no additional physical security.
- Identified possible strengths of Option 2:
  - only authorised users with recognised faces can be allowed onto the system
  - does not require users to remember/carry additional security identification.
- Identified possible weaknesses of Option 2:
  - system could be fooled by using a photo of an authorised user
  - software not 100% accurate so unauthorised users may still gain entry.

- Conclude with a discussion of which option may have the greatest impact, for example:
  – Option 2 is likely to be the most effective measure. The retailer will employ lots of computer users and Option 1 requires all users to use these measures correctly at all times. Option 2 does not require users to do anything except show their face when they wish to gain access to the system. Unauthorised users could still fool the software, but if they are additionally required to enter a valid password, then the system should remain protected.

Practice assessment 2

1 (a) Acceptable responses. Any **two** of the following, for example:
- virus
- worm
- trojan
- botnet
- ransomware
- rootkit
- spyware.

(b) Acceptable responses. Any **two** of the following, for example:
- SMS (text message)
- email
- social media message.

(c) Individual responses. Any **one** of the following, for example:

Accessibility features:
- display settings allow text to be increased in size, making text easier to read
- high-contrast display makes the text lighter and the background darker so that text is easier to read
- magnifier enlarges sections of the screen, making it easier to read
- narrator reads text on screen aloud so that Jack does not have to read it himself.

(d) Individual responses. Any **one** of the following, for example:

Information protection:
- sensitive information such as passwords could be hidden using *****
- sit with his back to a wall so that nobody can stand behind him while he works
- check that no one is standing behind him while he works
- close the screen/lock the screen when he is not working so others cannot see what is displayed
- ensure two-factor authentication is used to minimise the impact of a password being seen.

(e) Individual responses. Any **two** of the following, for example:

Impact of technology on an individual's well-being:
- may increase contact with others as you can chat online with people with similar interests
- may increase self-confidence as you can find out information to make you more knowledgeable
- may provide a relief from stress by playing online games/ watching videos
- may increase loneliness/anxiety due to too much time online and not enough time interacting with others
- may increase free time as less time may be spent travelling if working remotely
- may increase stress/anxiety due to blurring of boundaries between work and leisure time.

2 (a) Acceptable responses:
- grey hat (hacker)
- white hat (hacker).

(b) Individual responses. Any **one** of the following, for example:

Environmental impacts:
- more resources used because more computers will need to be built
- may create more waste because more products may be thrown away
- more energy consumed by digital systems manufacturers may contribute to climate change
- less electricity consumed because newer products tend to be more energy efficient.

(c) Individual responses. Any **two** of the following, for example:

Improvements to form:
- use a calendar to reduce risk of user entering an incorrect date of birth
- divide name into parts (for example, first, last) to ensure user enters all parts of name required
- divide address into parts (for example, town, postcode) to ensure user enters all required parts of address
- state who the contact number is for to enable user to enter appropriate details
- provide on-screen/pop-up help to enable user to understand how to complete the form correctly

(d) Individual responses. Any **two** of the following, for example:

A password policy will:
- encourage users to choose a strong password by defining the features of a strong password
- force users to change their passwords regularly by setting a period after which passwords must be changed
- increase data security by requiring users to change default passwords
- meet data protection legislation, for example, by protecting data with passwords that are hard to guess.

3 (a) Individual responses. Any **one** of the following, for example:

Poor network availability:
- mobile phone providers do not invest in infrastructure because there is generally a lower population in rural areas
- signal blackspots because of nearby mountains or hills.

(b) Individual responses. Any **two** of the following, for example:

Social media:
- can advertise the holiday cottage business, for example, by including photos and giving a link to its website
- may include positive reviews from guests, encouraging others to stay
- can communicate with potential guests by responding to questions/comments
- can stay in contact with guests through updates/news about the holiday cottages and facilities nearby
- can run promotions/adverts targeted at specific types of guest based on their social media profile/activity.

(c) Individual responses. Any **two** of the following, for example:

Email addresses:
- can allow a business to send out marketing information/ newsletters so guests may choose to stay again
- can be used to contact guests if any issues arise before they arrive, such as building work that may affect them during their stay

- can be used to set up a Wi-Fi account for the guests to use during their stay.

(d) Your answer should include a diagram with accurate labelling. Your diagram also needs to show connections and data flows and should accurately reflect the requirements of the question.

Possible top level (Level 0) data flow diagram:

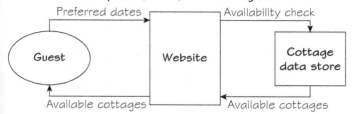

4 (a) Individual responses. Any **one** of the following, for example:

Levels of permitted access:
- specify (whitelist) the data to which writers have access
- allow access only to data relevant to the job role
- prevent access to confidential/non-relevant information.

(b) Individual responses. An explanation including any **one** of the following, for example:

Power-saving settings:
- a dimmer screen uses less energy, so less processing power is required and less energy needs to be generated to supply the business's power needs
- screens switch off quicker, so each device uses less energy overall and the business consumes less energy
- battery-powered devices need to be charged less frequently, so each device uses less energy and the business doesn't need to use so much energy.

(c) Individual responses. Any **one** of the following, for example:

Open Wi-Fi network:
- the document is at risk of being hacked/intercepted because the open network is unencrypted and data can be captured by a hacker
- the network is not secure because it is not encrypted and the document is at risk of being intercepted by an unauthorised user
- the company is not keeping documents as secure as possible, so personal data is at risk of being stolen; this could breach data protection regulations.

(d) Individual response. Your answer should show accurate and detailed knowledge and understanding. Your points should be relevant to the context in the question, with clear links. Your discussion should be well developed and logical, clearly considering different aspects and how they interrelate.

Your discussion may include some of the following points, for example:
- Track changes in word-processing app: used to ensure that any edits can be seen together with the replaced text. The lead writer or editor can then decide whether to accept/reject the changes made and ensure that there is a consistent approach to changes made.
- Comment tool: allows one writer to comment on the work of others. Effective use includes the use of helpful comments (for example, suggestions for improvement), rather than criticism of another writer's work without offering improvements.

- Versioning: use of version numbers to show which is the current and which is the previous version of a document. This enables all users to ensure that edits are made to the current version.
- Writers may be based in different time zones: writers should be sensitive to the working hours of colleagues in different locations. For example, they should not expect an instant reply from a colleague whose time zone is eight hours ahead/behind them.
- Real-time collaboration/shared editing rights: writers should explain any changes being made to a document as it may not be obvious to a colleague why a change is being made.
- Calendars/organisers: these enable meetings to be organised and other writers invited, and to-do lists and deadlines to be set and monitored.
- Video-conferencing/chat apps: these enable face-to-face or virtual discussions to take place in real time.
- Project-management discussion groups: if these are used in real time they may have to wait for colleagues in different time zones to return to their desks the next morning.

(e) Your answer should show accurate and detailed knowledge and understanding. Your points should be relevant to the context in the question, with clear links. Your response should be well developed and logical, clearly considering the different factors and their importance, leading to a supported conclusion.

Your evaluation may include some of the following points, for example:
- Possible benefits of online apps:
  - no need to install software on devices
  - no need to maintain/update software
  - reduced storage capacity needed for devices
  - no compatibility issues between devices.
- Possible drawbacks of online apps:
  - require always-on internet connection
  - increased risk of data-hacking
  - potentially higher cost to use the service.
- Possible benefits of cloud storage:
  - reduced need for own back-up storage services
  - reduced data storage needed for devices
  - reduced risk of data-hacking
  - easier to work using different devices
  - can support remote working.
- Possible drawbacks of cloud storage:
  - cost of using service (businesses will pay)
  - requires internet connection
  - requires service provider to be providing security/back-up of data.
- Conclusion should include a justified recommendation as to which proposal will have the greatest positive impact on the business. For example:
  - Cloud storage will be better because it reduces the need for the business to organise its own back-ups and means it will suffer less damage if a disaster occurs that makes its buildings and equipment unusable.

Practice assessment 3

1 (a) Individual responses. Any **two** of the following, for example:

Benefits of cloud storage:
- The company's data is saved automatically.
- The company's data is stored off-site.
- The cloud storage provider is responsible for backing up the company's data.
- The company may have access to some free cloud storage.
- Data can be accessed by multiple (authorised) employees.
- Data stored may still be available when employees are offline/not connected to the internet.
- Cloud data can be accessed by employees from any location with an internet connection.
- The service is scalable, meaning the amount used can be increased or decreased as required by the company.
- The company does not need to purchase or update data storage devices/servers.

(b) Individual responses. Any **two** of the following, for example:

A cloud services provider can:
- offer the company security of data
- provide services that are compatible with the company's digital systems
- be responsible for maintenance issues
- offer speed of access
- be responsible for resolving performance issues
- offer value for money/provide their services at a reasonable cost
- offer tools that enable collaborative working.

(c) Individual responses. Any **two** of the following, for example:

Use of mobile phones:
- Employees may be unable to make/stick to plans for their free time if contacted by their manager.
- Employees are responsible for keeping devices charged outside working hours.
- May increase employees' workload.
- May increase employees' stress levels.
- May disrupt employees' family/social life.

(d) Individual responses. Any **one** of the following, for example:

To protect against ransomware, the company may:
- use anti-virus software to detect and delete any ransomware downloaded onto the system
- prevent staff from using portable storage devices, such as USB drives, as they can contain ransomware
- use a firewall to block access to untrusted websites as they may contain malicious software
- use a firewall to prevent unauthorised incoming network traffic as this may be a malware attack
- train staff in the safe use of the internet/email to prevent ransomware being accidentally downloaded
- ensure that security/operating system software is up to date.

(e) Individual responses. Any **two** of the following, for example:

To reduce environmental impact, the company could:
- purchase devices that use recycled materials, so fewer resources are extracted to make the devices
- use low-energy devices, so electricity consumption is reduced
- use power-save settings, so devices switch more quickly
- replace devices less often, so fewer devices are purchased/made

- distribute all documents electronically, so fewer resources are consumed.

2 (a) Individual responses. Any **two** of the following, for example:

Use of cookies:
- A cookie can store the content of a shopping basket, so the user is more likely to complete booking a class if, for example, their session is interrupted.
- A cookie can be used to display targeted advertising, meaning the leisure centre can make more money by selling advertising space.
- The leisure centre could receive more bookings for fitness classes, because the cookie could be used to display information that is relevant to the user's own personal fitness interests.

(b) Individual responses. Any **one** of the following, for example:

Breach of copyright:
- The copyright holder could request the leisure centre to stop using the image, or else be taken to court.
- The leisure centre could be taken to court for breach of copyright and may have to pay a fine to the copyright holder.
- The copyright holder may demand that the leisure centre pay them a fee to compensate for the failure to request permission to use the image.

(c) Individual responses. Any **two** of the following, for example:
- Data must be collected for a specified purpose – no purpose is specified.
- Data collected must be relevant and necessary – the form asks for information that is not relevant or necessary (annual income/social media accounts).
- Data captured for one purpose (membership of the leisure centre) must not be used for other purposes – the form states that information may be used for unspecified other purposes.

(d) Individual responses. Any **two** of the following, for example:

The company may use private communication channels to:
- send confidential information that only the specific member needs to see
- help ensure that data protection requirements are met if the data subject's personal information is transmitted
- have a discussion with a specific member that it was not necessary for other people to see.

3 (a) Individual responses. Any **one** of the following, for example:

Restrict access to patient information:
- locate digital system/servers in a locked room that may only be accessed by authorised users with key/electronic lock
- secure PCs to a desk with a cable lock to prevent theft
- use passwords to prevent unauthorised users from logging on to the system
- use biometrics to deny access to someone whose fingerprint/iris scan isn't recognised
- use two-factor authentication to deny access to anyone who cannot verify their identify using their smartphone.

(b) Individual responses. Any **two** of the following, for example:

Actions following a cyberattack:
- investigate the nature/severity/extent of the attack
- respond by informing customers and relevant authorities, such as the police, of the attack

- manage/contain the attack (shut down affected systems), and preserve evidence of the attack in case of a criminal investigation
- recover by restoring systems
- analyse lessons learned to protect against any future attack.

(c) Individual responses. Any **two** of the following, for example:

Failure to provide equal access:
- Patients with a different type of smartphone operating system would not be able to use the app.
- Some patients may be unable to travel to the medical centre, due to their location or physical needs.
- Patients may suffer from unequal internet access, due to poor network coverage or limited mobile data plans.

(d) Your answer should include a diagram with accurate labelling. Your diagram also needs to show connections and data flows and should accurately reflect the requirements of the question.

Possible flow chart:

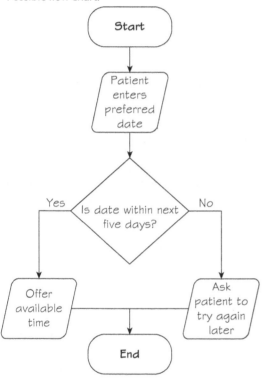

4 (a) Individual responses. Any **one** of the following, for example:

Penetration testing:
- An ethical hacker tests the system's security using a range of social engineering and cyberattack techniques.
- Any weaknesses found are noted, and included in a report to the theme park.
- The ethical hacker reports weaknesses and recommends improvements to the park's security.
- The theme park implements the hacker's recommendations to improve the system's security.

(b) Individual responses. Any **one** of the following, for example:

Web-based software:
- The theme park could save money because they do not need to pay to install software, and therefore don't need to pay for a software licence.

- The theme park does not need to worry about the software being out of date; they do not need to install any software because it is accessed directly from the cloud computing service.
- Staff can work from anywhere using any device because they do not need to have any software installed, apart from a web browser.
- Also, the employees could collaborate on projects more easily, because web-based software such as word processors allow multiple people to access/edit a file in real time.

(c) Individual responses. Your answer should include a correct reason, a justification for that reason, and an expansion of the justification. For example:
- communication between two devices is intercepted, and the interceptor may alter the contents of the message and then steal the information exchanged by the two devices.

(d) Individual response. Your answer should show accurate and detailed knowledge and understanding. Your points should be relevant to the context in the question, with clear links. Your discussion should be well developed and logical, clearly considering different aspects and how they interrelate.

Your discussion may include some of the following points, for example:
- use of assistive technologies to enable users with accessibility needs to work effectively, such as tools to improve visual display
- use of technologies to support older workers who may have age-related needs
- use of technologies to support home working to enable workers with health-related needs to work
- use of technologies to support remote working to enable workers to manage their professional life alongside their personal responsibilities; to enable workers living in remote locations to work for the theme park; to enable people from different countries and cultures to work together.

(e) Individual response. Your answer should show accurate and detailed knowledge and understanding. Your points should be relevant to the context in the question, with clear links. Your response should be well developed and logical, clearly considering the different factors and their importance, leading to a supported conclusion.

Your evaluation may include the following, for example:
- Possible benefits of anti-virus/firewall software:
  - improved data security
  - reduced chance of hackers accessing data, for example, by installing viruses
  - reduced chance of data loss, for example, by viruses corrupting files
  - firewall prevents incoming data from entering the network unless in response to a user's request.
- Possible drawbacks of firewall/anti-virus software:
  - does not eliminate all risk, for example, may not prevent phishing attacks
  - anti-virus library must be kept up-to-date.
- Possible benefits of data encryption:
  - data is unreadable by third parties unless they have a correct decryption key
  - reduced chance of information in files being read if the data is intercepted.

- Possible drawbacks of data encryption:
  - can slow down data transfer
  - requires all users to have encryption/decryption software installed and working correctly
  - may require passcode/security key to operate – this needs to be kept secure by all users.
- Conclusion – this should recommend and justify which proposal will have the greatest positive impact on the theme park. For example, data encryption is better. Although anti-virus and firewall software will reduce the risk of data being intercepted, if it is, then the hacker will be able to access the theme park's information. If data is encrypted, then it is very unlikely that the hacker will be able to view the information.

Practice assessment 4

1 (a) Acceptable responses:
- Assign tasks to individuals.
- Set deadlines for tasks.

(b) Individual responses. Any **one** of the following, for example:

Acceptable use policy:
- Scope – who the document applies to/what it covers/when it came into effect.
- Assets – what equipment/information/data the policy covers.
- Behaviours – defines acceptable/unacceptable behaviours/hardware/software/data use from employees.
- Monitoring behaviour – describes how the organisation monitors individuals' behaviour.
- Sanctions – describes how the organisation will deal with any breaches of the policy/defines minor and major breaches/the sanctions it can impose, such as warnings or dismissal.

(c) Individual responses. Any **one** of the following, for example:

Strong password:
- A mixture of different characters, such as numbers or special characters, increases the range of characters that need to be guessed.
- A hard-to-guess phrase makes it less likely a hacker will be able to input the same phrase.
- Random characters that do not contain any guessable strings, such as words or number sequences, means that easy-to-guess words will not feature in the password.
- More than eight characters increases the possible number of character strings/phrases that the password could contain, making it harder to guess.

(d) Individual responses. Any **one** of the following, for example:

Using several different servers:
- any data deleted on one server is still available on another, making it less likely that data will be lost
- quicker to recover from a disaster, as data is backed up in several locations.

(e) Individual responses. Any **two** of the following, for example:

Open Wi-Fi network:
- No password is required to join the network so anyone can set up a hotspot and use it to collect data from users.
- Open networks are usually unencrypted, so data sent can be read by anyone able to access the network's traffic.
- Unencrypted data can be intercepted, so a 'man-in-the-middle' attacker could steal data.

2 (a) Individual responses. Any one of the following, for example:

Alt text:
- provides a description of the image/video
- can be read aloud by the screen-reader
- enables the user to hear a description of the image.

(b) Individual responses. Any **one** of the following, for example:

Negative comments on social media:
- The reputation of the streaming service may suffer, so customers may be less likely to use the streaming service in the future.
- The streaming service may have to spend time and money repairing the damage to its reputation.

(c) Individual responses. Any **two** of the following, for example:

Music search form:
- give more emphasis to the title, such as using bold or a larger font size, to make the purpose clear
- include a drop-down menu for year of release to make searching easier
- include a drop-down menu for genre to make searching easier
- provide help/instructions to enable the user to understand how to complete the form correctly
- include search option to enable the user to input their own choice
- provide navigation features to make navigation easier
- provide accessibility options/features to improve the service for different abilities.

(d) Individual responses. Any **two** of the following, for example:

The streaming service:
- is able to compete with other similar services because net neutrality stops individual companies gaining an advantage by negotiating faster download speeds with the ISP
- can potentially reach all internet users because net neutrality prevents ISPs blocking its services in preference to other companies
- can compete fairly with all other streaming services because net neutrality stops ISPs from charging extra to their customers who wish to use the streaming service
- net neutrality stops ISPs from dictating which websites their customers visit so the ISP must allow them to use the streaming service if they wish.

3 (a) Individual responses. Any **one** of the following, for example:

Internal security threats:
- An employee could visit an untrustworthy website, causing data-collecting malware to be downloaded.
- An employee could respond to a phishing email and so disclose security information, such as username and password, enabling a hacker to obtain data.
- An employee could download software from the internet that contains viruses which collect data.
- An employee could use a portable USB storage device which contains malware that is then installed on the digital system.
- An employee could use a portable USB storage device to copy files from the system to give to a rival business.
- An employee could shoulder surf a colleague and use their username/password to access restricted data which they then steal.

(b) Individual responses. Any **two** of the following, for example:

Software tools (user access restriction):
- A firewall will restrict movement of data in and out of the system/will only allow incoming data that is trusted/

requested.
- Anti-virus software will protect the system by detecting/blocking malware, such as viruses, trojans and rootkits.
- Two-factor authentication requires a user to enter two different types of security information, at least one requiring them to have access to a separate device.

(c) Individual responses. Any **two** of the following, for example:

Legal requirements:
- The business should use the information for the purpose for which it was collected, for example to provide details of the nearest store.
- The information should not be shared with organisations that do not need to comply with equivalent legal requirements, for example, those based in countries without adequate data protection legislation.
- The information should not be stored for longer than is necessary, for example, it shouldn't be used to track a person's movements over a period of time.

(d) Example flow chart :

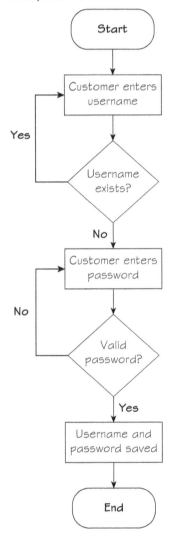

Solutions may use other relevant phrasing/wording in a flow chart. The flow chart must use correct logic and should produce the expected outcome.

4 (a) Individual responses. Any **one** of the following, for example:

Passwords:
- Hard-to-remember passwords are sometimes written down – a hacker could use this to gain access.

- Passwords can be forgotten, preventing the user from gaining access until the password is reset.
- Simple passwords can be guessed easily even if the hacker doesn't know the password.

(b) Individual responses. Your answer needs to include a correct reason, a justification for that reason, and an expansion of the justification. For example:
- Data is scrambled so anyone viewing the files is unable to understand the information without the correct decryption key.

(c) Individual responses. Any **one** of the following, for example:

Benefits of cloud computing
- Only one version of the file is created, so Tanya will always be using the most up-to-date version and time will not be wasted finding the right version.
- Tanya could use different devices at home and the office, so data security is improved because she does not need to take equipment out of the office when travelling home.
- Synchronising can ensure that the file is backed up to the cloud, so if there is a fault with one of her devices Tanya can continue to work on her documents using a different device.

(d) Your answer should show accurate and detailed knowledge and understanding. Your points should be relevant to the context in the question, with clear links. Your discussion should be well developed and logical, clearly considering different aspects and how they interrelate.

Your discussion may include some of the following points, for example:

A disaster recovery policy:
- reduces the disruption to operations caused by a disaster
- ensures key staff know what to do
- ensures all staff know what actions to take
- reduces the risk of loss of equipment/data
- enables back-up systems/data to be located and used quickly
- increases speed of response following a disaster
- enables the organisation to return to normal as quickly as possible after a disaster.

(e) Individual response. Your answer should show accurate, detailed knowledge and understanding. Your points should be relevant to the context in the question, with clear links. Your evaluation should be well developed and logical, clearly considering different aspects and competing points in detail, leading to a conclusion that is fully supported.

Your evaluation may include some of the following benefits and drawbacks, followed by a conclusion as to which option should be chosen:
- Identified benefits of Option 1, for example:
  - The software can run without the user's computer being connected to the internet.
  - The data created using the software will be stored on the user's computer unless an alternative storage location is selected.
  - The software is likely to load and run quickly as no data needs to be exchanged with a cloud computing provider.
  - The software will be the complete version of the software.
- Identified benefits of Option 2, for example:
  - Storage space is saved on the company's computers.
  - There is no need to manually update software as the online software will always be the most up-to-date version.

- There is no need to purchase/audit software licences.
        - Technical support staff time is reduced as less
          maintenance is needed, for example, to update software.
        - The cost of using the software can be spread over the
          life of the product.
- Identified drawbacks of Option 1, for example:
        - Technical support staff time is needed to maintain the
          software, for example, to install updates.
        - Licence(s) may need to be purchased when the software
          is first installed.
        - Not all users may use the software, so storage space is
          wasted on some computers.
- Identified drawbacks of Option 2, for example:
        - Users must be connected to the internet to use the
          software.
        - A poor internet connection will slow the speed at which
          work can be done.
        - Use may increase the internet bandwidth needed by the
          company (making internet use more expensive).
- Conclude with a discussion of which option should be
      chosen and why, for example:
        - The company should choose Option 1 if most of its
          users are based in its office and the business wishes
          them to have the most powerful version of the software
          available at all times.
        - Alternatively, it should choose Option 2 if many users
          travel away from the office, need to use the most up-to-
          date software features and have internet access.